10

Mrs Tibbs has left her shopping on Ben the Number Ten bus. But Ben can't take it to her – he has to make sure the children get to school on time. Then Ben meets Terry the Taxi. Will he be able to help?

BEN THE BUS

Mrs Tibbs' Biscuits

written by Sylvana Nown
illustrated by David Moss
from original designs by Albert Rusling

The right of Sylvana Nown and Albert Rusling to be identified
as author of this work has been asserted by them in accordance
with the Copyright, Designs and Patents Act 1988.
Copyright © 1990 World International Publishing Limited
All rights reserved.
Published in Great Britain by World International Publishing Limited,
An Egmont Company, Egmont House, P.O. Box 111,
Great Ducie Street, Manchester M60 3BL.
Printed in DDR. ISBN 0 7235 4494 8

A CIP catalogue record for this book is available from the British Library

It was a bright sunny day in the Strand. Ben
the Number Ten bus was happy to be out of
the bus shed and rumbling down the road.
He was carrying some children to school, a
few office workers who were reading their
newspapers, and some early shoppers, on
their way to the supermarket.

Inside, Clifford the conductor was walking down the aisle, whistling, when he saw a big blue bag on an empty seat.

Clifford stopped whistling. "Hello," he said. "What's this?"

He peered inside and found a jar of coffee, two cream buns in a bag, a packet of digestive biscuits and a bottle of milk.

"Oh no," Clifford groaned. "Mrs Tibbs has left her shopping again. She bought it specially, too, because her daughter is coming to tea."

He pushed back his conductor's cap and wondered what to do.

"She would forget her head if it wasn't screwed on," he said.

Clifford carried the bag to the front of the bus. He told Doris the driver what had happened.

"Bumpers," said Ben the Number Ten, looking bothered. "We haven't time to deliver Mrs Tibbs' shopping. We have to get the children to school."

Just then, Ben heard a familiar sound coming round the corner. It was his cheeky friend, Terry the Taxi.

"Move over," Terry hooted, pushing his way through the traffic. "Clear the way."

Terry was always in a hurry, even when he had nowhere to go.

"Over here, Terry," called Ben.

Terry crossed to the other side of the road and stopped with a squeal of brakes.

"Hello, hello," beamed Terry. "What's the problem, then?"

"It's poor Mrs Tibbs," said Ben. "She left all her shopping on one of my empty seats. And her daughter is coming to tea."

Clifford explained the problem to Tony the taxi driver.

"Deary me," frowned Tony. "We can't have that. Where does she live?"

"In those tall flats on the other side of the park," said Clifford.

"Well, pop the shopping in our boot," said Tony cheerfully. "We'll deliver it later."

"Must be off now," Terry called to Ben. And away he went, flashing his lights, pushing his way into the traffic and hooting his horn. He was always in a hurry.

I do hope he gets to Mrs Tibbs' flat in time for tea, thought Ben as Clifford jumped aboard and rang the bell.

When Ben pulled up at the next stop, Mr Wibberly, the bus inspector, was waiting, looking at his pocket watch.

"Now then, now then," said Inspector Wibberly, striding towards Ben with his hands behind his back. "What's all this?"

Oh dear, thought Ben. Whatever's wrong now?

Inspector Wibberly had to make sure that all the buses ran on time. When they didn't, he could be very cross indeed.

"One minute five seconds late," said Inspector Wibberly, looking stern.

"We're terribly sorry," Clifford apologized. "But Mrs Tibbs left her shopping on the bus."

"Not again," said the inspector, shaking his head. "We could open a supermarket with all the shopping Mrs Tibbs leaves behind. You will have to make up the time on your return journey."

Clifford reached up to ring the bell.
"Just a minute," said the inspector,
raising his eyebrows as he looked at
Clifford's jacket.

"What's wrong?" asked Clifford, puzzled.
"Your badge," Inspector Wibberly gasped. "Where is your conductor's badge?"

"Goodness," said Clifford, feeling his empty lapel. "It's gone."

The inspector pulled out his big black rule book.

"Here we are," he said, turning the pages. "Rule 174 — 'conductors cannot conduct a bus without a badge'. When you get back to the bus shed you will have to stay there for the rest of the day."

"But how will the children get home from school?" asked Clifford.

"Not my problem," said the inspector, closing his book. "Rules are rules."

And away he went.

On the way back to the bus shed Clifford searched everywhere for his badge. On the top deck. On the lower deck. Down the back of the seats. On the stairs. Under the stairs. But the badge was nowhere to be found.

When they reached the bus shed, Clifford told Doris that he could not find his badge anywhere.

"We'll have to stay here for the rest of the day," thought Ben glumly. "The children will have to walk home from school."

At that moment Ben heard Terry the Taxi coming round the corner.

"Move over, move over," Terry called to the other cars. He was in a hurry as usual.

I do wish he would slow down a little, thought Ben.

"Hello, hello," Terry called cheerfully. "Did you manage to give Mrs Tibbs her shopping in time for tea?" Ben asked. "Only just," smiled Terry.

Tony, his driver, got out of the taxi grinning. "Mrs Tibbs was so pleased that she gave me tea and biscuits," he told Clifford. "I was munching away at those digestive biscuits when I bit into something very hard. And when I looked, it was..."
Tony held up a large white disc.

"My badge," shouted Clifford in delight.
"It must have fallen into Mrs Tibbs'
shopping bag when I gave her a ticket."
Ben smiled and twinkled his lights.
"Quickly, Clifford," Doris said. "If we
leave now, we'll be in time to pick the
children up from school."

Clifford jumped on to the platform and
rang Ben's bell.

"Thank you, Terry," Ben called.

Ding, ding! went the bell.

And off they went.